Blood of Our Earth

# Blood of Our Earth

## Poetic History of the American Indian

**DAN C. JONES**
*Sa Su Weh of the Ponca*

**Artwork by Rance Hood**

UNIVERSITY OF NEW MEXICO PRESS

ALBUQUERQUE

10  09  08  07  06  05     1  2  3  4  5  6  7

LIBRARY OF CONGRESS CATALOGING-IN-PUBLICATION DATA

Jones, Dan C., 1951–
    Blood of our earth : poetic history of the American Indian
    / Dan C. Jones (Sa Su Weh, Ponca, author's native name
    and tribe);
    artwork by Rance Hood.—1st ed.
        p. cm.
            ISBN 0-8263-3810-0 (pbk. : alk. paper)
    1.  Indians of North America—Poetry.
    I. Title.
        PS3610.O623B58 2005
        811 .6—dc22
                        2004021291

*Special thanks to Ray and Velma Falconer*
*for their photograph collection*
*and for keeping the memories and history*
*of my family and fellow tribesmen alive.*

DESIGN AND COMPOSITION: *Mina Yamashita*

# Poems

Poems speak of thoughts
that one may see
through another person's eyes.

Poems may speak of the places
others have never been.

Poems bring feelings to share,
in a time when people need to care.

# Contents

# Part II
# Blood of Our Earth is Sacred

31

## CHAPTER I
## Beautiful Dreamer Awakens to the Real Earth / 31

## CHAPTER II
## God's Country / 55

Blood of Our Earth

x   Blood of Our Earth

# FOREWORD

*The Blood of Our Earth* is best understood by knowing something of where I came from. I was born and raised on the Ponca Indian Reserve in Oklahoma. My great-grandparents, Sam and Esther Little Cook, were on the Ponca Trail of Tears. They settled on allotted lands in what was then Indian Territory. My mother was born on these same lands in a teepee, in 1913. The Poncas were caught in a whirlwind of change. Outside influences were using Ponca resources to build vast fortunes and to come to international prominence, leaving the Poncas clinging to their culture and little else. At the same time the United States government actively dismantled our culture by using Boarding Schools to replace Ponca language and culture with English and American. My grandmother, Elizabeth Little Cook-Pensoneau, was taken from her family at four years of age to Chilocco Indian School, where she lived for eighteen years of her life. Her three sisters escaped that fate and received the blue circular tattoo on the forehead that was the symbol of "The Bringers of Life" literally, daughters of a Ponca Chief.

In 1879 Colonel George Miller, retired military officer, followed the Poncas to their new reservation of 101,850 acres in northern Oklahoma to establish what became the famous Miller Brothers' 101 Ranch and Wild West Show. In just a few years he was able to control nearly all of the Ponca Reserve by lease agreements that later turned into deeds. Many Poncas became reliant on the 101 Ranch for its general store and for providing jobs. Many Poncas became showmen in the 101 Wild West Show, traveling the world performing as Indians from the wild west, attacking stagecoaches and participating in the parade as trick riders and dancers dressed in

Facing page: Three of four sisters, the author's great-aunts (from left to right: Fannie, Annie, and Creth Little Cook).

Ga-hi-ge, or "The Chief," born in 1836 (photo taken in 1877).

Ponca Indian performer clowning with 101 painted on his face.

Velma Pensoneau, the author's mother, while working as a secretary to Zach Miller for the Miller Brothers' 101 Ranch and Wild West Show.

The 101 Wild West Show traveled the globe. The troupe became the talent resource for the first films made in Hollywood.

traditional regalia. Some Poncas had other special talents used in the show, such as my great-aunt Julia Big Snake-Paden who was the Fat Lady, a full-blood who weighed nearly 600 pounds at the time of her death. She was known to cowboy and Indian alike as difficult if not impossible to handle because of her incredible strength. The Miller family built an empire for two generations on Ponca Lands. Colonel Zack Miller, land baron and showman extraordinaire, took over the leadership of the Ranch. My mother, Velma, was his secretary. Pretty and educated, she was no one to mess with as she strolled the streets of Ponca City with her pet badger on a leash. Many Poncas took part in the first films ever made. Early Hollywood filmmakers used the Wild West Show's talent to make the first Westerns that started it all. Today Poncas are

Julie Big Snake-Paden at 600 pounds.

Top, left: Ponca warriors portray a dramatic reenactment of a stagecoach robbery.

Top, right: Ruth Duncan (7' tall) with Zach Miller Jr. and a Ponca Indian boy.

Bottom, left: Ponca trick riders' stunts were crowd pleasers.

Bottom, right: George Eagle; Stack Lee, sharp shooter and boomerang expert; White Eagle, a Ponca Chief; W. S. Prettyman, photographer, took most of the photographs reproduced here.

still active in film and television. I am a member of the Producers Guild of America, one among a few American Indians.

Others came and created vast fortunes at the expense of the Poncas, such as the oil baron E. W. Marland who founded the Marland Oil Co., but lost his company through his dealings with the powerful J. P. Morgan. He started Continental Oil that later became Conoco and later was owned by Dupont Chemical Corporation. Today it is Conoco/Philips. Marland's first oil well was called the Willie Cry #1 on the Cries-For-War Allotment. Marland wrote about how lazy the 101 cowboys were as oil rough necks as he ate his lunch while sitting on Ponca tombstones at the Ponca Cemetery adjacent to his first well.

*The Blood of Our Earth* represents five years of traveling to various Indian reservations throughout America and Canada and demonstrates a philosophy of the earth that comes from a people who believe they are not separate from, but bonded with all of its elements and creatures.

*The Blood of Our Earth* seeks freedom from all forms of oppression, freedom that can only come from love for one another, from asking for spiritual guidance, from self-awareness, from the pursuit of knowledge and values, and from cultural revitalization for the Ponca. According to Paulo Friere, the greatest danger would be to become so familiar with the tools and weapons of oppression, regardless of how subtle or violent, that we skillfully use them on one another.

In deep appreciation to Brenda Chergo and Dennis Michael Jones for making these works possible and to Rance Hood for seeing the vision; also to my mother and father who passed down to me a sense of the meaning of history and of the importance of searching for knowledge.

—DAN C. JONES
SaSuWeh of the Ponca
Ponca City, Oklahoma, 2004

Ponca delegation to Washington D.C., 1910.

# Part I
# Blood of Our Earth
# Is Shed

## CHAPTER I

## From the Blood of Our Earth

# From the Blood of My Earth

I speak to ones that should know, but don't.
I speak of what I saw
when a restless mind enters no sleep,
I fell into a vision.

I saw great leaves that carried men
that floated to shore from the sea.
They brought love, then they brought disease.
All were painted white, and each carried a long knife
when put to his shoulder made loud thunder.

The thunder killed all the birds of the skies.
It killed all the fish of the water.
It killed all the animals of the land.
It killed my mother and father.
The smoke from the long knife filled the heavens
even killing the men painted white.

A fire started in my stomach.
It made me vomit clouds of smoke.
I threw myself on the ground eating handfuls of dirt.
As I lay there burning,
I saw a man leave my body.

He stood there taking all the air from the heavens
into his lungs, and when he released it
it was pure again.
He did the same with the earth,
and it was pure.
He did the same with the waters and
they too became pure.

As he walked away, in his footprints,
in every step he took, sprang a pool of blood.
Each pool of blood grew into a kind of animal
or a tribe of people,
each a different color.
All rose to form one great nation
that glowed of youth and warmth
that I knew, had become pure
from the blood of my earth!

# When We Die

When we die
our bodies do feed this earth.
When you walk upon this earth,
do ever so lightly please.

We are of this earth.
When you hold the earth
you feel the spirit
we have shared.

Know this,
many of us have come and gone
before you or your father were.
We are the same as the earth.

So when you walk upon the earth
you walk upon us.
Feel this earth and know
we are still here.

# In a Time Long Ago

In a time long ago
I left my people
to follow the cycle of the sun,
to find those who speak
in wisdom and truth.

In my travel
I would meet ones
who in their greed would claim
what rightfully belongs to all
that grows, walks or crawls.

In a burning thirst I asked for water.
The white man returned with fire.

# Who's Laughing

The coyotes are laughing.
Dogs are senselessly barking,
aimlessly running,
all while coyotes are laughing.

Cows are grazing, waiting for the slaughter,
eating more than they put on the table,
while buffalo bones
bleach in the sun.

White men build dams.
He stops the great rivers—
while the salmon
are waiting to go home.

These are signs of a man
who has lost his balance.
Men who lose their balance
will fall.

Buffalo bones bleach in the sun.
Salmon are waiting to go home,
all while
coyotes are laughing.

# City Streets

There comes to me once in a while
walking these city streets,
the call of the wild.

Oh and my blood runs free,
stalking the plants that feed me,
the smell of the city sickens me,
the liquor leaves me empty,
a hollow shallow feeling.

I can't seem to help myself
but to drink it
for it does take my heart and head
far from this damn city.

# That Sunday Afternoon

I guess I've wasted my time
with those lonely thoughts of you.
It's close till two,
last call on a Saturday night
as I watch them go home, two by two.
It makes a lonely feeling feel worse
going home alone with them lonely thoughts of you.

When you took my children away
that Sunday afternoon,
you took a piece of me.
As the years pass by, the wounds heal to scars.
It don't hurt so bad now,
to see you come and go,
but when you take my boy,
and he says: Daddy I'll miss you,
I break down and cry.

When a man can't even walk in the sun
because its warmth reminds him of you,
it's a damn, black Sunday afternoon.
Guess I'll go down to the bar
where it's black and cold
try to drink it away
pass out in the back
on a damn, black Sunday afternoon.

I lost your love, but that boy loves his dad.
I see it in his eyes when he cries
when its time to leave.
It's damn black Sunday afternoon.
I'll get up in the afternoon to go down again,
with those lonely thoughts of you,
on a lonely, black Sunday afternoon.

## The River

I saw your rivers flowing.
They looked to be flowing blood.
I see visions in my mind
of clear water flowing still.

Oh brother
Walk not hard on
because the mud is
quick and the
water is
deep
and
you
might
drown!

## The Race

He longs for peace and joy.
Hard looking, still waiting,
he longs for peace and joy.
Tired of a world filled with
violence, war and crime,
it makes his life weary.
Still yet sadder, he's just a young man
with so long to go.
He longs for peace and joy.

World with no face, you're staring at me.
World with great ears, you need none.
World with no face, turn toward the sun
till you blister and bake, then burn.
World with no face,
death must be your pay for living.
World with no face, you're nameless,
so I'll name you, the damned human race.

Backward people of a backward race
running a backward race,
trying to get somewhere
backwards at a forward pace.
Pushing, shoving, running over,
kicking, stomping, screaming people,
all backwards.
It's such a ridiculous race.

## America

America don't you feel me?
I'm your Native people's son.
America, don't you see me?
I'm the one with the sun in his heart.
My Mother is of the Earth
My Father is of the sky.
America, don't you know me?
I'm the one you've taken my Mother from.
I'm your Native people's son.

## Stumbling Man

The foolish man is a mad dog
that would bite the hand that feeds it.
He has pitted himself against nature,
a foolish man's war
with no reason.
A stumbling man
with all his great wisdom,
when loses his balance
will fall.

Ned Little Hoe, Ponca Spiritual leader.

CHAPTER II

# Men Did Walk This Way
# Before the Horse Was Rode

# My Travels

In my travels
as the earth moves below my feet,
like turning the pages of a book
in a child's hands.
It soothes the wild man,
causes dreams that change things
and the artist that's within me
comes alive.

To strive to copy the Creation,
in my dreams this brings me closer
to our Creator.
This is good for me
I can erase the bad things,
paint over the sad things.

18  Blood of Our Earth

## Lady Montana

Oh lady Montana
I look upon your beauty,
it sets me to my knees
yet fills me with an emptiness.
For I feel the ghost images
of all the animals you've slaughtered.

Oh Montana,
What will it take to make you feel
the space that you defouled?
I speak for the animals you have slaughtered;
We are now pushed to the steepest ridges
of the highest mountains.
We beg you stop the call
for men to come, to pay you,
to slaughter us.

I speak now for the animals
and this is what they had to say:
Oh Montana,
we pray to God
you set the world to reason.
Do not send men here to kill us,
for we are inseparable with the earth.
For when we are gone,
these mountains will crumble
as heavens tears,
they will wash all men away.

# The Trapper

Cold chills do make us shudder
as we hear the screams of men in pain.
I wish to write no sad song,
but this I feel I must.
I've heard animals cry the same.

The cold wind chill that I now
breathe through your ears,
the cold wind has taken the lives
of many a trapper.
And I'm sure they died in vain.

Does the sound of animals screaming
twist their young ones' hearts with pain?
For I am sure they died in vain.
Now this is one thing I know,
animals do have feelings
like us, it is almost the same,
for I have heard them scream in pain.

So is it not strange a twisted man would torture an animal
to twist its mind in pain?
Now do not get me wrong.
Nature is sometimes cruel in her ways.
Men do have a right to use the hides of over-populated animals
for they might die anyway.
They will provide warmth for your family.

Now to those men of greed—we know who they are.
Has not nature taught the true value of life,
that all things in nature are sacred?
I do curse you now with the spirit of all animals in pain
so you may know how you are.
So the life of our animals
was not in vain.

# The Dream

I knew from stories told,

men did walk this way

before the horse was rode.

Yes the wind does cry way up here,

pray or die.

I knew from the bones far below,

from the ground,

the mountains tops covered with mist,

that the wind swirls

like spirits taking form.

From the depths far below my reaches

thoughts come forth of pictures

of me falling, falling,

and the winds cry, pray, pray or die.

I fall, the wind cries.

I call God's name.

There's a gentle shake.

My eyes open to a familiar face that says,

Awake brother, it's time to hunt.

# In Search of the Wily Wapiti

The message was not quite clear
but it did say, it was a dangerous trail.
The message was heard in the wind.
Do not laugh my friend.
There's lots of lost souls under slippery rock.
To you that don't understand I said:
There's a path to take that's called Dangerous Trail
where many men and animals fell
over slippery rock to Dangerous Trail.
When even the wind laughs then cries and says:
pray or die, it's best to listen my friend.

In the north country of Montana
Blackfeet Indian country,
Big Badger river winds its way to the great divide.
It's a gateway—gateway to the wilderness.
There's a trail there across slippery rock
where many men and horses fell, as story tell,
over slippery rock to Dangerous Trail.
Many visions fill one's mind when on this trail,
of Indians and mountain men.
The Indians pray for safety over slippery rock.
The bones of those who did not pray, still lay
far below to the bottom of the steep canyon,
the bones of horses and mountain men.
Even the wind whispers, pray or die,
in search of the wily wapiti.

The spirit of the wind laughs then cries.
The message is the same, pray or die.
We feed our children wild meat to keep them strong.
As bad off as things are, we are strong.
Do not misunderstand me,
we dare not disturb the balnce for trophy.
We have learned much from Our Mother, the Earth.
We see her in balance
as kind as she can be cruel.
Hunt with wisdom, hunt in balance,
hunt to feed the people.
If your path is a dangerous trail,
ride with no fear,
in balance God rides with you,
in search of the wily wapiti.

DAN C. JONES  25

# Handgame

A whirlwind begins the war
as tribes meet.
Drums roar, rattles shake, snakes strike,
Night Gun shoots, Good Eagles soar,
two sticks, two sticks,
the crowd goes wild.
Good Eagles fly, Good Eagles hide,
Night Gun shoots, Good Eagles dive.

Billy Goat's the one as he waves his wand.
He calls the bones and they come,
two by two.
The crowd goes wild
as drums roar, rattles shake,
snakes strike, sparks fly.

Night Gun shoots, two sticks, two sticks
Good Eagles soar, again.
Those Blackfeet are running away.
In the night or light when they hide,
they seem to disappear.
Night Gun shoots, bones fly,
the crowd goes wild
as drums roar, rattles shake, sparks fly.

Someone new to the war can clearly see
this has been done before.
You can see spirits of souls
gone long before, still playing.
You can see from the spirit of the game
it will be for a long time to come.
Drums roar, rattles shake,
snakes strike, sparks fly.
A whirlwind begins the war
as tribes meet.

## Seeds

Our Mother

this earth

is full of the blood

of our ancestors.

From the blood of our earth

comes the spirit

that causes new seeds

to grow

the old way

strong again.

Yellow Buffalo, Ponca.

# PART II
# Blood of Our Earth is Sacred

## CHAPTER I

## Beautiful Dreamer Awakens to the Real Earth

# Beautiful Dreamer's Song

The beautiful Dreamer's Song
Awakens us to the real earth.
The song is carried to the Four
Winds—so that all people may
                    Hear.

There is warning in the song. It
says . . . Speak only of what you truly
know. Walk softly upon the earth.
All men's actions are recorded. We
do stand responsible for what we
                    Say.

Too long men have been telling us
We are the impossible dreamers, and
they the conscious masters. That the
earth is here to rape. Turn away
from these men quickly. Death is their
pay for living. For the Spirit that
protects all living things is now
                    With us.

The Whip-poor-will sings his name.
This is right. It is so right that birds
sing songs. It sounds right. They must
know what they say. Men should take
this as a lesson. When they speak they
should know what they say. Otherwise it
                    Is nowhere.

They call us impossible dreamers
because we dream of living with the
land to feed ourselves. The earth feeds
us. We know that. Yet to ask children
where bread comes from, they tell you
the grocery store. Who's really the
                    Impossible dreamer?

The earth clothes us with the wrapper
of the meat, hand tanned buckskin. We hunt
the weakest to let the strongest multiply
their strength. Nature taught us
this from the wolf. Men taught us
this from the wolf. Men taught us to
hunt the strongest for trophy. This is
a mad dog that
                    Would bite the hand that feeds it.

This earth is our home. Our shelter
comes from the trees, the trees
from the forest. The forest is the
home of many many kinds of life.
Yet when you ask most loggers
what they see when they look at
the forest, they say trees. Who's
the Impossible Dreamer?
                    Who sees realities?

Nature's laws are the flow of energy
that keep people in harmony with
all that surround you. God's rules
for people to deal with the earth,
to keep this earth healthy, strong for
                    Future mankind.

Time is God's measure for people.
So people may measure their
Spiritual progress in their life.
Know life is a test. We were created
for fellowship with All-mighty God
who is perfect. Keep this in mind.
For shortly, the righteous will live on
earth in the paradise,
                    It is meant to be.

# Since Time Began

Since time began

warriors roamed this earth.

Like buffalo, they moved in cycles

Yet unlike all other animals,

for they were masters,

proud caretakers of a beautiful land,

though humble servants

of a greater being.


Their reason for being is sound.

They are linked to the master plan.

You can't destroy them

without destroying yourself,

for like the buffalo,

they have reason for being here.

And they were created by God.

## Remember Your Ways

Remember your ways.
In a time when all seems lost—
it's not.
I speak from both sides now,
but in the end, all will know
survival is the greatest gift of all,
to the people
and a very gifted people you are.

The wheel of life has left
much power in the face of your old ones.
Turn to them and know
all is not lost.
Go to the sun,
speak God's name
in your native peoples tongue.
In a time when all seems lost—
it's not.

DAN C. JONES 37

# Direction

Direction—a search for settlement,
in a very unsettled time.
Like a search for peace
in a time of war.

In a time this country is changing
as quickly as turning the pages of a book
in a child's hands.
Many dangers cross our path each day.
We face new obstacles that seem impossible.
When we pray for strength,
our prayers are answered for the load seems lighter.

For a young Indian seeking direction
or which path to follow—
the white man's or the Indian's,
the young man must think,
if he takes the white man's road,
take only the paths that are
good for people and kind to nature.
But what the young Indian must remember,
is when he becomes an old man,
he will still be an Indian.

# When a Warrior Feels Weak

When a warrior feels weak,

I think of the strength in a bee

when he chases a bear from his home.


When a warrior feels weak,

I feel no loss of strength

when I think of the sparrow

that attacks the eagle.


When a warrior feels weak

I become aware of my strength.

42  Blood of Our Earth

# Teepee Knowledge

Ah, has the thought ever crossed your mind
how the Natives of America
knew their exact boundaries
and were able to travel great distances
with great accuracy,
without fear of becoming lost?
There are many examples of what I speak of.
Even in traveling unmarked territory,
never the fear of becoming lost in the wilderness.
If you've ever been in the wilderness,
you know of what I speak.
Yes as masters of this land
their teepees were as ships,
and hold this secret of navigation.
As no ship is without a sextant
to be guided by the stars.
The teepee itself is a sextant within itself,
directly aligned with the heavens
so to exactly map the Earth.

# Survival

To survive a great storm,
you have to know in your mind
that your shelter is held
by a force far greater
than the wind itself.

And in these times
the key to survival is—
follow the energies that move you
and let your heart be your home.

DAN C. JONES  45

# The Warrior

'Tis fall of the year.

Autumn's artist has carefully painted

each tree,

and fallen leaves

have painted the earth.

Looking down into a clearing in the woods

we see a herd of deer

before, we see standing by a tree,

as carefully painted

as mother nature has painted each tree,

he blends so well, so hard to see

even the deer overlook him.

Stands a warrior with bow and arrow pulled taut.

He has studied the herd

and knows his mark at the weakest,

for he knows nature well

and dares not upset the balance for trophy.

Listen to the song his heart sings his mind

as his mind prays to his Creator.


A cool breeze swirls the leaves

like pools of paint,

time for a warrior to provide for his family.

A humble man of wisdom and strength

guided by eternal spirits,

as kind to nature

as a pure mountain stream.

## Fish People

Living here in the beauty
of the fish people's ways,
my travels have brought me
a new perspective
on life and its creatures.

For one thing
the Red Man is and will be
the true caretaker of this land
after the purification
and into the new world.

For his heart is good,
his mind is strong,
for all that he's been through
his sense of survival
is surpassed by no one.

## River Spirit

The spirit grows weary Great One.

This mind has refused to sleep.

In this condition I find comfort

in one of your creations Great One.

For your river spirit is strong

and great and he never sleeps.

## Fish People II

Somehow, in a way
I don't really understand,
being only a visitor
to the fish people's land.
I see in the order of the fish
a balance so delicate and sensitive,
it makes good reason to honor
this greatest of great gifts
from the Creator,
to my friends,
in the ways of the fish people.

50   Blood of Our Earth

## Medicine Man

To hear a song of nature sung true,

believe me, it's a moving song to me.

It moves me to hear

the song of a medicine man.

It brings pictures in my mind

of true men living still,

crying, praying for all that is,

for all that will be.

How thoughtful these men must be.

Do you know what I say

when we talk of the medicine people

and their gentle ways?

Well, when you hear one sing his song

you'll know what I mean

to hear a song of nature sung true.

Believe me,

it's a moving song to you.

## Gentle Warrior

Whispering gentle words of wisdom

Attacks with the speed of a thought,

Hits the heart with the power of thunder!

With eyes of an eagle,

Sight of an arrow in flight,

Wisdom carries truer than strength.

Making the wise man the stronger,

The strong man the wiser,

So is the way of the gentle warrior.

I speak to ones that should know

but don't.

DAN C. JONES 53

Little Soldier and his three wives.

# CHAPTER II

## God's Country

## God's Country

What ever makes me uneasy,
What ever makes me sad,
When I know this is God's country
and I am here now.

## The Feather

The feather for its weight
is the strongest structure
in all of nature.
How easy it crumbles
in the wrong man's hands,
who holds no birds
as being special.

The teachings of Christ, so simple,
yet the strongest words of all of nature.
How easy they crumble
in the wrong man's hands,
who holds no teaching
as being special.

## The Sweat Lodge

Though my synagogue is made of willow
it is worth more to me than gold.
Though time has come and passed
like leaves, our kind
did Fall winds scatter.

Like us, as mulch,
I feel our warmth will cause
new seeds to grow strong again.
In as much as my synagogue
is made of willow
it is worth to me
more than gold.

## Master of the Sun

Master of the sun
don't leave me.
Master of the sun
bring all your children home.

Living the beauty of life
brings me closer to You
            my home
                one
we are all one.
Master of the sun
bring all your children home.

Master of the sun
you feed me
Energy.
We are all one.
Master of the sun
bring all your children home.

## Morning's Win

Warm the earth below my feet

Soft the touch to my bare feet

Sweet the smell

God's nectar, honey suckle

Cool the feel of sky's pure dew

Cool the air it quickens the thought

Beautiful the sound

of thoughtful Creator's creatures

As we awaken

to morning's win

over black night's shroud.

# Gentle Rain

Gentle rain marks this a new day.
As sad clouds weep,
new grass laughs.
What is it this feeling with us
who are caught between
this season of tears and laughter.

New rain falls,
washes the old snow away.
It makes deer happy
to see new plants grow before their eyes
On a warm spring day
with rain amid the mountains,
the new young play,
while my thoughts are of you so far away,
be happy I pray
for springtime makes all things new again.

Sad clouds weep, new grass laughs,
starving elk may feast again,
for their young have no sorrow
for their grass is green again.
Though the snow hid the ground for so long
they never forget the grass
that will be green again.

## Bury Me in the Willow Tree

Passing days,

like falling leaves

one by one

till one day a whirlwind

leaves us bare trees

bending in the wind.


Weep for me too, willow

and pray for the earth

that has fed us so well

for so many years,

and sing that our bodies

feed her in the end.